Understanding Iran™

# IRAN'S
# RELIGIOUS
# LEADERS

ROSEN
PUBLISHING
New York

M. Shapera

*For Adam Shapera*

Published in 2010 by The Rosen Publishing Group, Inc.
29 East 21st Street, New York, NY 10010

**Library of Congress Cataloging-in-Publication Data**

Shapera, Paul M.
Iran's religious leaders / Paul M. Shapera.—1st ed.
    p. cm.—(Understanding Iran)
Includes bibliographical references and index.
ISBN-13: 978-1-4358-5283-9 (library binding)
1. Iran—Politics and government—1979–1997. 2. Iran—Politics and government—1997– 3. Islam and state—Iran. 4. Islam and politics—Iran. 5. Iran. Majlis-i Khubragan. I. Title.
DS318.825.S535 2010
955.05'4—dc22

                                                    2008047709

*Manufactured in China*
**On the cover:** A group of Iranian clerics recites verses from the Qur'an at a weekly Friday prayer service in the Iranian capital city of Tehran.

# Contents

# Introduction

On the morning of February 1, 1979, more than one million Iranians gathered at the international airport of Iran's capital, Tehran. Another five million crowded the streets of the surrounding city, waiting for a certain plane to touch down. Inside the plane was an Islamic cleric, Ayatollah Ruholla Khomeini. When he stepped off the plane, the city erupted in celebration. A blue-and-white car slowly drove him through the crowd of people, finally arriving at the Cemetery of Martyrs, twelve miles (nineteen kilometers) south of Tehran. There, he addressed his supporters, saying, "I will

Some of Iran's leading clerics, members of the Assembly of Experts, meet in Tehran on September 4, 2007, to elect a new chairman.

strike with my fists at the mouths of this government. From now on it is I who will name the government."

Iran's shah, or king, had fled the country fourteen days earlier. The prime minister he appointed just before leaving cautiously watched Ayatollah Khomeini's arrival. The government stood practically helpless after an entire year of riots and strikes. Within ten days of his arrival, Ayatollah Khomeini made good on his promise. His most loyal supporters stormed the government buildings, putting an end to the shah's government. Ignoring all of his nonreligious allies, the ayatollah proclaimed the dawning of a new era in Iranian history, an Islamic republic. Clerics, that is, religious figures, would now rule the country and ensure that every aspect of Iranian life would follow their careful interpretation of Islam.

This book will look at the events surrounding the 1979 Islamic Revolution. It will examine the powerful clerics who replaced the shah and the government they formed. Finally, it will look at the policies they put into place that continue to shape and define Iran to the present day.

# Chapter One
# Islam

In order to understand the clerics who control the Iranian government, one must understand their beliefs—the religion of Islam. Islam is the second-largest religion in the world, numbering an estimated 1.2 billion followers. The word "Islam" means "submission to God" in Arabic. Those who believe in Islam are known as Muslims, meaning "those who submit to God." Islam was started in the seventh century CE by the

Iranian Muslims attend prayer and a sermon at Tehran University on December 31, 2006.

prophet Muhammad. He is the one whom Muslims consider to be the last and the greatest prophet ever sent by God. Muslims believe that Muhammad did not invent Islam but instead brought about a return to the original true religion preached by all prophets before him.

## The Prophet Muhammad

Muhammad was born in 570. His parents died when he was very young, leaving him to be raised by his uncle. He grew up in the city of Mecca, which is located in the country now called Saudi Arabia.

As an adult, Muhammad would often leave the city and go to the nearby mountains to meditate and pray for days or even weeks at a time. According to Islamic beliefs, when Muhammad was forty years old, the angel Gabriel appeared to him while he was praying in a small cave. Gabriel spoke to Muhammad, delivering to him a message from God (Allah). Muhammad memorized the message and eventually recited it, word for word, to his small group of followers. Gabriel continued to appear and deliver these spoken messages periodically for the rest of Muhammad's life. These revelations from the angel were written down in the Qur'an, the Muslim holy book.

Muhammad tried to tell others about these revelations and convince them that God had appointed Muhammad as his messenger. However, few people in Mecca believed him. At the time, most Meccans were polytheists, meaning they worshipped many gods. They became hostile toward this preacher and his small group of followers, and in 622, Muhammad and

# The Qur'an

The Qur'an is the most holy book of Islam, made up of the recitations revealed to Muhammad by God during Muhammad's life. As the direct word of God, the Arabic text of the Qur'an is considered sacred. For this reason, there are special rules Muslims need to follow when handling the Qur'an. For example, Muslims should be facing the direction of Mecca if reciting from it and should not handle the Qur'an without washing their hands, or sometimes showering. The Qur'an is organized into 114 suras, or

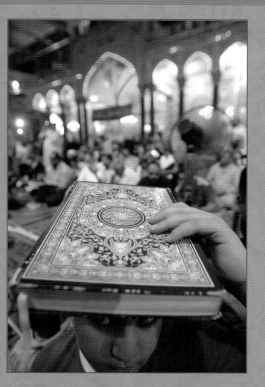

A Shiite Muslim boy places the holy Qur'an atop his head as he recites prayers during a service commemorating the murder of the prophet Muhammad's nephew, Ali.

chapters, of various lengths. These contain the basic beliefs of Islam, its practice, and its law. The scriptures provide careful explanations of right and wrong behavior for everyday life as well as various social, political, and economic activities.

his followers were forced to leave the city. They fled to the nearby city of Medina. Muhammad was welcomed in Medina because he was well known there for his sense of fairness. Warring tribal parties in Medina wanted him present to help them in a series of disputes they were having. Muslims mark the year this happened as year 1 on their calendar.

In Medina, Muhammad's preaching received a warmer welcome. Many heard his sermons, and in just a few years, the number of his followers grew to ten thousand. Meanwhile, the city of Mecca had seized the property of the Muslims who had departed with Muhammad. The exiled Muslims responded by raiding Meccan caravans, or traveling parties. This eventually led to open warfare between Muslims and the residents of Mecca. The Muslims won, and by 630, the city that had forced Muhammad to flee was in Muslim hands. Soon, almost the entire city was converted to Islam. The new religion proved to be a very powerful tool of social organization. Over the next several centuries, Muslims spread out and conquered the entire Middle East, northern Africa, central Asia, and areas of Spain and India. In this way, Islam became one of the largest religions in the world.

## Islamic Faith

Islam has six articles of faith. An article of faith is a statement that describes a basic belief held by a member of a religion. There are two important groups of Muslims, the Shia and the Sunni. Iran is mostly made up of Shia (approximately 90 percent of the country is

Shia). We will pay particular attention to their beliefs.
A Muslim must believe in:

- One god, whose name is Allah.
- Angels, who are divine beings serving
  God's will, such as the angel Gabriel, who
  recited the Qur'an to Muhammad.
- Four holy books, of which the Qur'an is by
  far the most important. The other three
  books are the Torah (the first five books of
  the Old Testament), the Injil (the Gospel of
  Jesus), and the Zabur (the Psalms of King
  David). Muslims believe that these last
  three books have been changed over time
  so they are no longer as true and pure as
  they once were. This is why God needed to
  deliver the Qur'an to mankind.
- Prophets. Muslims believe that faith in
  God comes naturally to human beings but
  that people nevertheless lose their way
  and fall into false beliefs. Allah therefore
  sends messengers, or prophets, to remind
  humankind of what true faith is. Muslims
  believe that Allah has spoken through
  many prophets, including Adam, Noah,
  Abraham, Moses, and Jesus. Their last and
  greatest prophet of all is Muhammad.
- A day of judgment, when every person
  who has ever lived will stand before God
  and be placed into either heaven or hell.
- Divine justice (*adalah*, in Arabic). The Shia
  believe that part of God's plan is divine

justice. They believe that everything in the world is either good or evil and that God has commanded humans to choose only the good.

In addition to what Muslims believe, there are certain things all Muslims must do. These are called the Five Pillars of Islam. They are:

- *Shahadah*  Attesting that there is no other god but Allah.
- *Salat*  Praying five times a day facing Mecca.
- *Zakah*  Giving to charity.
- *Sawm*  Fasting during the holy month of Ramadan.
- *Hajj*  Journeying to Mecca at least once in a person's lifetime.

All Muslims abide by these first five pillars of faith. The Shia have additional articles of faith:

- *Khums*  A 20 percent tax on a Muslim's profits or treasures.
- *Jihad*  Struggling against sin.
- *Tawalla*  Love and devotion for the prophet Muhammad's family.
- *Tabarra*  Rejection of anyone who is an enemy of the Prophet's family. This was important in historical times, when hatred of the Prophet's family usually resulted in their assassination.

Muslims gather at the Grand Mosque in Mecca, Islam's holiest city. Every Muslim is required to perform the *hajj*, a pilgrimage to Mecca, at least once if they are able to do so.

- ***Amr bil ma'ruf*** Encouraging others to do good deeds.
- ***Nahi anil munkar*** Discouraging others from doing bad deeds.

## The Sunni and the Shia

Muslims have long been divided into two main groups, the Sunni and the Shia. This split occurred shortly after the prophet Muhammad's death in 632. After Muhammad died, it was unclear who should lead the Muslims and become the caliph, or successor of

Muhammad. Some Muslims believed that both God and the Prophet had named Muhammad's nephew, Ali, as the new caliph. He was pious and worthy of the title. Other Muslims argued that any devout Muslim could be caliph, and they favored Abu Bakr, Muhammad's father-in-law and one of his first converts. Despite this disagreement, Muslims finally agreed on Abu Bakr, and he became the first caliph.

About twenty years later, the fourth caliph, Uthman, was murdered while praying. Ali finally became caliph. But Ali faced serious difficulties. Both Muhammad's wife and Uthman's cousin, Mu'awiya, accused Ali of not being willing to track down and capture Uthman's killers. They demanded he step down as caliph. Ali refused and war broke out. Eventually, Ali was forced to declare a truce with Mu'awiya, but this so angered some of Ali's followers that one of them murdered him.

## Ramadan

Ramadan (or Ramazan) is the ninth month of the Muslim calendar. Ramadan is believed to be the month in which the angel Gabriel first appeared to Muhammad. During Ramadan, fasting (sawm) is prescribed. The fast begins at dawn each day. Until sunset, Muslims are prohibited from drinking, eating, smoking, and sexual activity. This time is an opportunity for Muslims to reflect on their faith. In addition to fasting, Muslims are encouraged to recite the whole Qur'an during this sacred month.

From this moment on, the Islamic world was divided on the question of authority. Mu'awiya became the fifth caliph. His clan, the Umayyad dynasty, continued to pass the caliphate down among its family. The followers of Mu'awiya came to be called Sunnis. There was a separate Islamic community that remained loyal to Ali and recognized only his descendants as the true authority. They gave this line of successors the title of imam—meaning "spiritual leader of Islam." These followers are known as Shias.

The divide between Sunnis and Shias continues to this day. Despite their disagreements, each group usually sees the other as part of the same wider Muslim community. Sunnis make up about 80 percent of the general Islamic population, and Shias make up about 20 percent. The large majority of Iranians, about 90 percent, are Shia. Shias also have large populations in Lebanon, Iraq, and Pakistan.

## The Twelfth Imam

The Shia followed the descendants of Ali, referring to their leaders as imams instead of caliphs. They believed that only the imam was capable of perfectly understanding all aspects of Islam, as well as being the wisest ruler of Muslim society. They counted Ali as the first imam. In 873 or 874, their eleventh imam died, leaving his five-year-old son, known as the Mahdi, to be the twelfth imam. However, almost immediately after his father's death, the Mahdi mysteriously disappeared. Many Shias chose to believe that the Twelfth Imam was not murdered or kidnapped but instead was mysteriously

Muslim women light candles at the height of Shabaniyah. This festival celebrates the birth of the Twelfth Imam, Mohammed al-Mahdi.

hidden by God. These Shias came to be known as Twelvers, or Ja'fari. They believe this hidden imam, the Twelfth Imam, will one day return to the world and establish a perfect and just era of Muslim civilization throughout the world. Until this day comes, all Muslim leaders are merely acting as substitutes in his place.

Iran was conquered in 1502 by a fifteen-year-old Shia leader. At that time, the country switched from Sunni Islam to Shia Islam. Iran's ruling clerics are Twelver Shias. They often discuss the coming of the Twelfth Imam.

## Chapter Two
# The Shahs of Iran

F or more than 2,500 years, Iran was ruled by kings usually referred to as shahs. Instead of being elected, most shahs were dynastic rulers, meaning they inherited the throne from their fathers before them. Others came to control the country through military conquest. Iran—or Persia, as it has been called in the past—was ruled by many shahs throughout its long history. In 1979, however, its history of monarchy ended with the

Mohammad Reza Pahlavi, the shah of Iran, sits on his elaborate, gem-encrusted throne, in March 1968.

Iranian Revolution. The last shah of Iran, Mohammad Reza Shah, was forced to flee the country, never to return. The next two chapters look more closely at the Iranian Revolution and the major figures and events that preceded the overthrow of the shah. This story begins at the end of World War I, in the early 1920s.

## Reza Shah Pahlavi

The Ottoman Empire was a great Muslim empire centered in Turkey. It dominated the Middle East for centuries. During World War I, however, the Ottoman Empire was overthrown. Britain, which played a key role in the Ottoman defeat, was eager to have more control over the region. In particular, the British wanted access to Middle Eastern oil, which they needed to fuel their highly industrialized economy.

Iran was troubled. There was no strong government, and gangs terrorized the cities. In the countryside, wandering nomads with tribal chieftains and rich landowners with large estates fought over small slices of territory. The shah no longer held power over the government. This job was the responsibility of the prime minister of Iran, but he, too, was unable to keep the peace. He recruited a colonel from the army, Reza Pahlavi, to impose order.

Reza Pahlavi had joined the army as a poor villager. However, he fought hard as a soldier, taught himself how to read and write, and eventually rose up the ranks to become colonel. After being hired by the prime minister, Reza realized that he could use the military under his control to seize power for himself.

Reza Shah Pahlavi is shown here dressed in his military uniform in 1910, fifteen years prior to becoming shah of Iran.

That is exactly what he did. In February 1921, Reza Pahlavi forced out the helpless prime minister and became the new shah of Iran.

Reza Shah used the military to put an end to the lawless situation in Iran. He succeeded in creating a stable government and unifying the country. He wanted Iran to become a modern nation, like the European nations of Great Britain, France, and Germany. In his quest for modernization, he fought hard to crush any opposition. This included the country's Muslim clerics.

Reza Shah established the foundations of a modern economy, with improved communication and transportation systems. He promoted rights for women, created a modern school system under the protection of the state (instead of clerical control), and built roads and factories. The shah wanted Iran to have a modern outlook on the world, and he felt that strict adherence to religion held back the nation.

Reza Shah was credited with a host of accomplishments in rebuilding and strengthening Iran. However, his practices did leave many Iranians dissatisfied. One issue was with the shah's large appetite for money. He bought vast tracts of land for himself by forcing regular people to sell it to him at very low prices.

Another huge issue Reza Shah faced was that the British still controlled the oil in Iran. This made the British a lot of money—profits that Iranians felt should belong to them.

Perhaps the greatest reason many Iranians disliked the shah was his ruthlessness toward anyone who spoke out against him. He was known to torture, imprison, and even kill his critics. Also, many Iranians were proud of their Persian heritage and wary of adopting the ways of European foreigners. Many still followed Islam with deep devotion. They resented Reza Shah's dismissive attitude toward both Islam and the clerics who preached it.

## Reza's son, Mohammad Reza Pahlavi

When World War II broke out, Reza Shah aligned Iran with Nazi Germany. He hoped that the Germans would defeat Great Britain and end British control over Iranian oil. But Germany was defeated, and Reza Shah was forced to resign. His son, Mohammad Reza Pahlavi, was put on the Iranian throne with the approval of Britain and its strong new ally, the United States of America.

Mohammad Reza Shah ruled in a similar way to his father. He, too, wanted to make Iran more modern. His plan to do so was called the White Revolution. Just like his father, Mohammad Reza Shah wanted Iran to resemble

A portrait of Mohammad Reza Pahlavi, from the 1950s

Europe and have modern industries, technologies, and fashions. He, too, wanted to weaken the influence of the Islamic clerics and would not tolerate disagreement. Like his father, he was quick to jail, torture, exile, and even kill his critics. He kept tight control over the newspapers and media, and just like his father, he accumulated a great deal of wealth.

In 1951, a popular politician named Mohammed Mosaddeq was elected prime minister of Iraq. Soon, Mosaddeq had gained enough popular support to threaten the shah with a revolution. The shah, fearing Mosaddeq supporters would kill him, fled

Premier Mohammed Mosaddeq delivers a speech in Majlis Square, Tehran, in September 1951. Extremely popular, he would soon overthrow the shah.

the country. When Mosaddeq assumed power, one of the first things he did was to take control of Iranian oil away from the British. This greatly upset the British, who asked the United States government for help. For their part, the Americans feared that Mosaddeq would build stronger ties with their Cold War enemy, Communist Russia.

With British support, the U.S. Central Intelligence Agency (CIA) organized a coup, known as Operation Ajax. A coup occurs when the government or leader of a country is removed by force. The Americans assembled a small force of guerrilla fighters within Iran, bribed key Iranian military officials, and secretly organized street protests. It was a complex plan,

## The White Revolution

The White Revolution was an ambitious countrywide program intended to modernize Iran. Launched in January 1963, it included massive land reforms, in which land was redistributed in order to build new factories, develop agriculture, construct roads and highways, and build and populate new villages. Many former landowners were given shares of the new state-owned industries in exchange for their land. Additionally, new rights were extended to women, such as the right to vote. Education and health services were brought to rural villages. Many new industries were also introduced, including steel production, oil refineries, hydraulic dams, ports, electrical power, and even automobile production plants.

resulting in the overthrow of Mosaddeq and the shah's return to the throne. Mosaddeq was given a quick trial and placed under house arrest until the end of his life in 1967.

Knowledge of this operation gradually leaked out, and the Iranian people seethed in anger. The idea that a foreign country would come in and secretly overthrow a popular elected leader was unforgivable. And the more the United States and the shah collaborated, the more the Iranian people came to resent them both.

Upon his return, the shah continued his practice of brutally silencing his critics. His powerful secret police organization, the SAVAK (Sazeman-e Ettela'at va Amniyat-e Keshvar), was feared for its cruelty. In order to make way for new streets, the shah demolished homes and neighborhoods without the consent of the homeowners. Villagers were forced to sell their farmland, and entire villages were destroyed or relocated in order to make room for modern factories. While there were wealthy businessmen who supported the shah, they were the minority. The gap between rich and poor grew wider and wider.

The clerics were bitterly opposed to the shah, not only for these land policies but also for his friendly relations with the United States and Israel. Clerics also opposed his liberal women's rights policies. Further, in urban areas, more and more young Iranians were taking part in such Western pastimes as gambling and drinking. As a result, the clerics equated the shah with the erosion of Muslim values. The country was headed toward a breaking point.

# Chapter Three
# The Iranian Revolution

espite the shah's attempts to silence his critics, some still spoke up. One of the loudest and most popular critics of the shah was a cleric named Ruholla Mussaui Khomeini.

## The End of the Shah

Ruholla Khomeini had risen to become ayatollah, a high position among Muslim clerics. Ayatollah Khomeini had

October 9, 1978—In downtown Tehran, enormous crowds gather for a demonstration against the shah.

been exiled from Iran in 1964 and was living mostly in neighboring Iraq. This gave him an advantage of being beyond the shah's reach. Khomeini wrote widely read books and pamphlets attacking the shah and his policies. Cassette tapes of his passionate speeches were passed around and heard by Iranian citizens from all walks of life.

In 1978, the shah's government ordered a newspaper to write an article insulting Ayatollah Khomeini. In the city of Qom, where Khomeini had achieved his popularity, Muslim students marched in the streets in protest. Police were sent in to break up the protest. When the students refused to leave, the police resorted to violence, and several students were killed.

Across Iran, people organized mourning ceremonies for the slain students. Many of these ceremonies turned into angry riots. Once again, the police attempted to break up the gatherings, resulting in a cycle of more violence, more deaths, and more mourning ceremonies.

Clerics began organizing more demonstrations, drawing larger and larger crowds. During the demonstrations, they gave impassioned speeches and passed out pamphlets calling for revolution. The number of demonstrations increased across the country. Beginning in late 1977, the clerics had called for a series of nationwide workers' strikes. By the end of 1978, these strikes had crippled the country and demonstrated to the shah his loss of control. Industry in Iran ground to a halt. The Americans, recognizing the seriousness of the situation, urged the shah to leave the country.

The shah, sick from cancer and powerless, fled on January 16, 1979. Two weeks later, on February 1,

January 1, 1979—Demonstrators hold up a sign with a picture of Ayatollah Mahmoud Taleghani, another very popular militant religious leader who opposed the shah.

Ayatollah Khomeini flew into Iran and was greeted at the airport by an estimated one million Iranians. Ten days later, on February 11, Khomeini's supporters took over all the government buildings, signaling the final collapse of the shah's rule.

## Ayatollah Khomeini

Ruholla Mussaui was born in 1902 in a small village of Khomein, about 200 miles (322 km) south of Tehran. His family was able to trace their roots all the way back to the prophet Muhammad. He was dedicated to his religious studies, and in 1923, he

Ayatollah Ruhollah Khomeini sits in a garden in the outskirts of Paris, France, not long before his triumphant return to Iran.

began studying at an Islamic academy in the Iranian city of Qom.

During the time Mussaui spent in Qom, the first Reza Shah was beginning the process of modernization in Iran. Mussaui watched as many important clerics protested against Reza Shah, only to be arrested, jailed, beaten, and exiled. This left a lasting impression on young Mussaui. However, despite his disagreements with the shah, for many years Mussaui did not speak out in public. His religious leader in Qom, Ayatollah Boroujerdi, did not believe that clerics should be

## Israel and the Palestinians

The area that is now Israel had once been the Jewish homeland. Then, about two thousand years ago, the Jews lost the territory in a Roman invasion. From that time, the territory became widely known as Palestine. In the nineteenth and twentieth centuries, a group of Jews called Zionists argued for the reestablishment of a Jewish state in Palestine. By that time, the region was populated mostly by Muslim Arabs.

During the first half of the twentieth century, Jewish immigrants poured into Palestine, many fleeing widespread persecution in Europe. After World War II, tensions ran high between the Jewish immigrants and the native Muslim Palestinian population. The United Nations recommended that Palestine be divided in half. One half should be a Jewish state, the other half should remain a Palestinian state. The Zionists were elated and declared the creation of the nation of Israel. However, the Palestinians and many of their Arab neighbors were appalled. In 1948, a yearlong war broke out. Arab forces from Egypt, Jordan, Lebanon, Syria, and Iraq assisted the Palestinians, but in the end the Zionists won.

Muslim Palestinians who had been living in the conquered territory were forced to leave their homes. These events infuriated Muslims all over the world, including Ayatollah Khomeini. To this day, conflict exists between Israel and the exiled Palestinians, and violence between the two sides continues.

involved in political affairs. Mussaui was obliged to accept his decision.

By the end of the 1920s, Ruholla Mussaui had himself become an ayatollah. Following tradition, he took as his surname the town in which he was born, becoming known as Ayatollah Khomeini. When Boroujerdi died in 1961, Khomeini began to make his views public. As the shah began implementing the White Revolution, Ayatollah Khomeini preached extensively against it. He spoke out against the shah's policies, saying they were evil and encouraged moral corruption. He warned that Islam itself was in danger. Khomeini believed that the shah's efforts to modernize the country were part of a plot by Israel, the United States, and Great Britain to destroy Islam and dominate the Iranian people. Ayatollah Khomeini particularly disliked Israel because of what he perceived as the country's unlawful occupation of Palestine.

In 1964, Ayatollah Khomeini gave a speech in which he declared the Iranian government illegitimate. Anyone who supported its policies, he said, was a traitor. Within days, the police arrested Khomeini, and he was forced out of the country. He eventually ended up in the Iraqi city of Najaf, where he would spend the next fourteen years of his life.

Once in Najaf, a Shiite holy city, the ayatollah continued with his mission. He wrote books and essays discussing Islam and criticizing the shah's pro-American policies. His numerous speeches were recorded on cassette tapes. Copies of these cassettes were smuggled into Iran and passed from hand to hand and played in markets, shops, and private homes. Through his

This close-up of Ayatollah Ruhollah Khomeini was taken in 1978, about one year before the fall of the shah.

writings and these tapes, Khomeini grew very popular, despite being exiled.

As the shah's popularity declined, Khomeini became more and more influential. Numerous groups allied themselves with the ayatollah, despite some disagreements with his religious views. These groups ranged from pro-democratic organizations to communists and more moderate Muslims. Khomeini envisioned a government run exclusively by strict Islamic clerics, but he was careful not to advertise his opinions widely. He needed the support of many different Iranian groups and had no intention of alienating them.

On January 16, 1979, the shah was finally forced to flee. And on February 1, 1979, fourteen years after being forced to leave, Ayatollah Khomeini arrived back in Iran. Following a nationwide vote, Khomeini and his followers proclaimed a new government—the Islamic Republic of Iran.

April 1, 1979, was declared the "first day of God's government." Khomeini assumed his position as the country's Supreme Leader. Many of the nonreligious groups and organizations that had helped him overthrow the shah began to realize that Khomeini was not going to include them in the decision-making levels of government. The highest positions were reserved for conservative, or traditional-minded, Muslim clerics. Under Ayatollah Khomeini, Iran was to be made into a strict Muslim society, an Islamic nation that would operate in harmony with the Qur'an.

# Chapter Four
# Rule of the Clerics

With the Islamic Revolution, the clerics in Iran assumed direct rule over the country. Shiite religious figures filled major political offices, while the supreme power was concentrated in the hands of one man, Ayatollah Khomeini, who considered himself God's representative on Earth. After decades of being repressed, Iran's clerics were eager to flex their authority.

A small group of Iranian clerics passes by a woman outside of the religious school of Faizieh, located in the holy city of Qom.

## Who Are the Clerics?

The term "clerics" refers to Muslims who have studied
and been confirmed at an Islamic seminary sometimes
referred to as a madrassa. In Iran, the best-known
center of religious learning is Qom. This city of about
a million people is located approximately 100 miles
(161 km) southwest of Tehran. It has fifty-two semi-
naries in which students train to become clerics.
Training includes studying the Qur'an, Islamic law
(sharia), Muslim history, Islamic logic, and sayings
and deeds of the prophet Muhammad (*hadith*). At the
end of their training, clerics are expected to be experts
in religious thinking, as well as in such other areas as
law, science, and philosophy.

A cleric who shows excellence in learning and
gains the respect of his teachers as well as his followers
is eligible to earn the title of ayatollah. "Ayatollah"
literally means "Sign of God." It is an honorific title
bestowed on outstanding religious scholars in the
Twelver Shia branch of Islam. The city of Qom has ten
senior, or grand, ayatollahs. In Arabic, they are called
*marja taqlid*, meaning "sources of emulation." They
maintain strong influence in society and have the
privilege of collecting and distributing money from
charity (zakah) and religious taxes. Shiite clerics may
own property or businesses, and some become quite
wealthy. Also, unlike clerics in some other religions,
they are allowed to marry and have children.

Iran's clerics play an important role in the lives of
the people. The main task of the clerics is to preserve
Islamic faith in society and to interpret the Islamic law

as established in the Qur'an and other texts. Clerics also offer guidance to their followers on a range of issues, including marriage, divorce, business practices, and hygiene. They do so through personal communication, through *risalas*, or through fatwas. A risala is a manual covering a cleric's religious and legal views on basic Islamic duties. Risalas may address issues of everyday concern or more serious political matters. If something isn't covered in a risala, then the cleric is asked to give an additional opinion, or fatwa. In Shia Islam, a fatwa given from a marja taqlid (spiritual leader) is considered binding and must be followed.

In February 2006, Iranian foreign minister Manouchehr Mottaki insisted to the press that fatwas from Iran's religious leaders prohibit Iran from developing nuclear weapons.

In recent years, Iran's ayatollahs have started to communicate with their followers through the Internet. Today, hundreds of clerics have their own Web sites, and they enjoy great popularity among large portions of the Iranian people. Risalas are posted on these sites, and followers can e-mail religious questions, which the clerics will respond to.

## Three Major Categories of Clerics

Clerics in Iran generally fall into one of the three main schools of thought: conservatives, reformists, and, more recently, pragmatists. The conservative branch follows the teachings of the late Ayatollah Khomeini. Conservative clerics hold all the most important posts in the government and play a key role in making Iran's political and social policies. These clerics also aim to uphold the strict religious values in all aspects of Iranian life and have strong anti-Western sentiments. Clerics who are especially uncompromising are referred to as hard-line conservatives.

The aim of the reformist clerics in Iran is to relax aspects of Iranian religious and political culture. Some of the main concerns of reformist clerics are to ensure greater protection of human and civil rights, to enable greater freedom of the press, and to establish a more democratic process of governing. Compared to the conservative clerics, reformist clerics are more open to negotiations and conversations with Westerners.

For decades, Iran's conservatives and reformists have battled each other to determine the direction of the country. However, the two groups have been unable

## Sharia

Sharia (meaning "path" in Arabic) represents a set of Islamic laws taken from the Qur'an and other Islamic texts. These texts record the sayings and deeds of the lesser prophets, the sayings and deeds of the prophet Muhammad, early Muslim traditions, and the opinions and rulings of Muslim scholars. Sharia covers nearly every aspect of Muslim life—political and domestic, social and private. By its nature, sharia is not set in stone, so the laws are open to great debate as to how to interpret and apply them to various aspects of Muslim life.

to agree. This has caused Iran to come to a political standstill on many important issues. In light of this gridlock, a new direction has emerged—pragmatism. The pragmatist clerics are more concerned with Iran's failing economy than with social reforms. Like the reformists, they desire better relations with the West. Pragmatists tend to have support from Iran's middle class and businessmen. With the declining power of the reformists to enact change, this group is shaping up to represent a new direction in Iranian politics.

## The New Government

This section takes a closer look at the political organization in Iran, outlining the structure and functioning of the Iranian government after the Islamic Revolution.

In March 1979, Iran held a vote. On the ballot was one question—Islamic republic: yes or no. The country

The Iranian flag, officially adopted on July 29, 1980, waves in the air. The symbol in the center is made up of four crescents, spelling out the name Allah (A-L-L-H), with a sword in the middle.

overwhelmingly voted "Yes." Khomeini officially became its Supreme Leader. He set about creating a new government, with a new constitution. Like the U.S. Constitution, this new Iranian constitution would clearly state how government was to function and how laws would be made and enforced.

Over the summer of 1979, a panel of experts was elected to write the new constitution. A group of seventy-five people, at least fifty of whom were clerics, spent the next several months creating it. It was during these sessions that many of Ayatollah Khomeini's former allies realized that the clerics had no intention of letting them have any say in the new government. There were many arguments as they tried to get their voices heard, but in the end, the clerics prevailed. The 1979 constitution effectively changed Iran into a constitutional theocracy. In other words, Iran was now a nation in which religious figures—in this case, Muslim clerics—played a central role in its constitutional government.

The new Iranian constitution called for a complete reorganization of the state. It was changed to be in line with sharia, or Islamic law. Rather than professional politicians, clerics would control all aspects of government to ensure that sharia is always followed. With this arrangement, any serious criticism of the government can be seen as disobedience to Islam itself.

## Government Structure

The government is basically divided into the clerical branch and the political branch.

| **Clerical Branch** | **Expediency Council** | **Political Branch** |
| --- | --- | --- |
| Supreme Leader | | President |
| Guardian Council | | Parliament |
| Assembly of Experts | | Judiciary |

### Clerical Branch

The clerical branch, in which only clerics can hold posts, is more powerful than the political branch.

### The Supreme Leader

The most powerful person in the entire government is the Supreme Leader. This is the position Ayatollah Khomeini held from the time he formed Iran's new government until he died ten years later, in 1989. The next and current Supreme Leader after him has a similar name—Ayatollah Ali Khamenei. The Supreme Leader is appointed for life by the Assembly of Experts, which also reviews his performance. Women are not eligible to become Supreme Leader.

According to Iran's new constitution, the Supreme Leader has the final say in all of Iran's policies. He often suggests what these policies should be. He holds veto power, meaning he can refuse to pass any law or decision made by any other branch of government. The Supreme Leader controls Iran's military and can single-handedly declare war. He appoints and dismisses Iran's top judges, otherwise known as the heads of the judiciary. This gives him enormous influence over the Iranian court system.

The Supreme Leader controls all radio and television stations, deciding what they can and cannot broadcast. He heads a group called the Supreme National Security Council, which sends newspapers a list of subjects they are forbidden to discuss. This group also controls the Internet. Powerful filtering programs made by U.S. companies block a huge number of Web sites from appearing on Iranian computers.

The Supreme Leader also appoints six of the twelve members of the Guardian Council, the second most powerful branch of Iranian government. The

Supreme Leader Ayatollah Ali Khamenei addresses a Friday prayer service at Tehran University in 1998.

amount of power the Supreme Leader holds can hardly be overstated. However, there are times when even he finds himself ignored. Iran's recent privatization efforts are an example. To help stimulate Iran's failing economy, Khamenei has ordered many state-run businesses to be sold to private owners. While these businesses are draining money from the government, they are putting money in the hands of religious foundations, military institutions, and merchants. An aluminum factory in central Iran, for instance, provides jobs for relatives of local officials, and like so many other state-run institutions, simply never gets sold. Despite repeated urgings by the Supreme Leader, this order stubbornly remains unheeded.

## The Guardian Council

The Guardian Council is made up of twelve clerics. Six of these are appointed directly by the Supreme Leader, and the other six are recommended by the head of the judiciary. Members of the Guardian Council have two very important jobs.

The first task they perform is to carefully examine all the laws passed by the parliament and decide whether these laws are in accordance with sharia and the Qur'an. No law can be put into effect without the approval of the Guardian Council, giving it enormous political power, second only to the Supreme Leader. Members of the Guardian Council are often in opposition to the Iranian parliament, which has attempted over the years to create laws giving citizens more freedoms. The Guardian Council, almost always siding with the Supreme Leader, has time and again vetoed all of these attempts at reform.

The second task the Guardian Council performs is determining who is allowed to run for president. The council typically disqualifies the vast majority of presidential applicants, particularly ones who are not in line with their conservative Islamic views. Women have never been allowed to run for president. After reformist candidate Mohammad Khatami was elected in 1997 and went on to serve two terms, the Guardian Council was vigilant in ensuring that no reformists ran during the 2004 elections. Out of one thousand candidates who registered, the Guardian Council allowed only six to run.

## The Assembly of Experts

The Assembly of Experts meets only once a year, for a week, usually in Qom. This body is made up of eighty-six clerics, who are elected every eight years. They essentially supervise the Supreme Leader's decisions. To this day, they have never directly questioned a decision the Supreme Leader has made, but they are the only governmental organization that could do so.

In addition, the Assembly of Experts appoints the Supreme Leader. They officially appointed Ayatollah Khomeini in 1979, and ten years later when he died, they appointed the next Supreme Leader, Ayatollah Ali Khamenei.

As of 2008, the head of the Assembly of Experts is the cleric Ali Akbar Hashemi Rafsanjani. He is a powerful force in Iranian politics. Rafsanjani was

In February 2008, Ali Akbar Hashemi Rafsanjani, the head of Iran's Assembly of Experts, addresses the assembly. Rafsanjani is a former Iranian president.

president of Iran from 1989 to 1997 and is one of the most influential pragmatists in the country. He opposes some of the harsher punishments prescribed under current Iranian law. In addition, he advocates free-market economic reforms, as well as friendlier relations with the West. He and President Mahmoud Ahmadinejad are well-known rivals. As of 2008, Rafsanjani was also chairman of the Expediency Council.

## Expediency Council

In between the clerical and political branches of government is the Expediency Council. Made up of forty members, the Expediency Council acts to solve disagreements and settle disputes between the two branches of government. It was created in 1988 after disagreements between conservative clerics in the Guardian Council and reformists in the parliament ground Iranian politics to a halt.

In 2005, when Supreme Leader Khamenei approved a twenty-year government development plan, he appointed the Expediency Council to carry it out. This gives them the power to supervise the other branches of government. The council does not, however, interfere in the day-to-day operations of the government.

## Political Branch

In the political branch, regular citizens—not just clerics—can be elected officials.

## The President

The president is in charge of Iran's economy and the development of Iran's economic policies. The president is also the face of Iran around the world, visiting foreign countries, meeting with other world leaders, and delivering speeches. However, the power of Iran's president is limited. His decisions can be overridden by the Supreme Leader or the Guardian Council.

Ultraconservative Iranian president Mahmoud Ahmadinejad appears at his very first press conference after being elected in June of 2005.

In 2005, Tehran's mayor, Mahmoud Ahmadinejad, was elected president of Iran. He is notorious for his hard-line conservative views and his confrontational attitude toward the United States. His opinions are much more in line with the clerics of the Guardian Council and the Supreme Leader than those of his predecessors. Yet, he is known to attract criticism from senior clerics, too, mainly regarding his failure to revive Iran's slumping economy.

## The Parliament (Majlis)

The parliament, also called the Majlis, creates and passes laws. It is very similar to the American Congress or British Parliament in this respect. The Majlis is in charge of things such as ratifying treaties with other countries and approving the budget. All of its decisions can be overturned by the Supreme Leader or the Guardian Council.

There are 290 people in the parliament, all of whom are elected every four years. Women can be elected to parliament. (Their numbers are few, however. In 2008, only eight women were elected, all of them conservative.) Until recently, the Majlis has had numerous reformist members, which caused great tension with the conservative branches of the Iranian government.

Many Iranians have been voting for reformist candidates who pledge to make Iran a more tolerant society with better rights for its citizens. But these reformers are largely unable to pass the promised laws because of the Guardian Council and the Supreme Leader's power of veto. Frustrated, in the 2008 parliamentary elections, many reform leaders urged citizens not to vote in protest. This resulted in conservatives gaining control. As of late 2008, conservatives held 69 percent of the seats, while reformists held 16 percent.

## The Judiciary

The judiciary branch is the court system that holds trials, convicts criminals, and decides who is right and wrong in legal disputes. It is also responsible for the enforcement of laws. The head of the judiciary is appointed directly by the Supreme Leader and, thus, is usually a hard-line conservative.

In the judiciary, there are three different kinds of courts: the Public Courts, the Revolutionary Courts, and the Special Clerical Court. Criminal trials and disagreements between citizens are handled by the Public Courts. Crimes against the country of Iran or against Islam are tried in a Revolutionary Court. The Revolutionary Court has no appeals, meaning that all verdicts are final, including death sentences. The third

An Iranian man stands trial in the Iranian Public Court in Tehran for the murder of his business partner.

court is the Special Clerical Court, which tries clerics accused of crimes.

Most judges in the court system are clerics. It often happens that there is no jury and there are no lawyers at the trials, with the judge also acting as a prosecutor. Because of the amount of work a judge is responsible for—the preliminary investigations, the trial, and the final verdict—the legal system is often backed up, leaving many cases awaiting trial.

Because the judiciary is usually controlled by hard-line conservatives, tensions can often run high between the judiciary and the less conservative Majlis. Some Majlis members have found themselves on trial for comments they made on the floor of the parliament.

# Chapter Five
# Opposition to Clerical Rule

I ran's ruling elites do not always agree on all issues. Even at the highest levels, there is a fair amount of political infighting and power struggles. One of the key political battles in Iran today is taking place between the reformists and conservatives. The clerics within the Iranian government are almost entirely conservative, although clerics in general can be of either persuasion.

Three Iranian girls, wearing traditional coverings called chadors, wait outside a mosque at a pro-reform rally in Tehran in June 2001.

# The Reformists

The reformists are people whose vision for Iran is to become more democratic, with greater political tolerance, better rights for women, and better economic opportunities. Some of them had helped expel the shah during the revolution but were either ignored afterward or grew tired of Ayatollah Khomeini and his followers. Many reformists argue that instead of greater freedom and a more prosperous future, the revolution resulted in a weaker economy, fewer freedoms, and greater inequality.

In 1997, a reformist cleric, Mohammad Khatami, was elected president by a large margin—70 percent of the vote. Khatami's election signaled that the majority of Iranian voters were dissatisfied with the way the country was being run. Like Khatami, many of his followers did not wish to put an end to the Islamic Republic. They wanted the system to evolve into a more progressive, democratic, and tolerant society.

Khatami was the great hope for the reformist movement, but bringing about real changes proved difficult. The conservative clerics and their power to veto all reforms were impossible to overcome. Khatami did manage to make some reforms, mainly in the areas of economy and civil liberties. His landslide reelection in 2001 was a sign that the majority of Iranian people approved of the direction he was taking.

However, in 2004, when it came time for the next election, the Guardian Council made sure that no reformist was allowed to run for president. They

Mohammad Khatami, a reformist and former president of Iran, urges Iranian citizens to vote in the 2008 parliamentary elections.

refused applications from anyone deemed not sufficiently Islamic. As a result, only six out of one thousand applicants were allowed to run. The next president of Iran was Mahmoud Ahmadinejad. As a hard-line conservative, his positions were more in line with those of the Supreme Leader and the Guardian Council.

In recent years, the reformist movement has been increasingly frustrated by the reversal of the changes brought about during Khatami's presidency. The activities of reformists have been heavily restricted, and the harassment of known reformists and journalists has increased.

One of the most prominent reformist critics is the senior cleric Grand Ayatollah Montazeri. Initially, Montazeri was a great supporter of the Islamic Revolution and the late Ayatollah Khomeini. However, many of his views later in his career put him at odds with the conservatives. He criticized the government for human rights abuses and the regime's poor management of the war with Iraq in the 1980s. He questioned the absolute authority of the Supreme Leader and was quoted as saying, "There is a great distance between what we have promised and what we have achieved."

The reaction by the conservative clerics was unforgiving. His political career was ruined, his private college was shut down, and he was placed under house arrest, allowed to see no one except his family. His memoir, published on the Internet, was denounced by conservatives, and some of his followers were arrested for their role in the memoir's preparation. Despite being heavily suppressed, Montazeri still communicates with his followers through the Internet and continues to issue fatwas to his many supporters. Scores of other reformists, including clerics, writers, economists, and others have suffered similar—or worse—fates under the conservative clerics' regime.

## Changing Attitudes

In 2004, the movie *The Lizard* was released. Iranians flocked to see it before it was banned in some areas. In the movie, a criminal named Reza steals a cleric's robe to escape from prison. In his new identity as a man of God, Reza encounters endless contempt from the various people he comes across. The movie represents a comedic look at the social restrictions imposed by the Iranian government. It also points to the increasingly wide rift between the general population and the ruling clerics.

After the revolution, clerics passed strict laws regarding all aspects of social life. Dress codes are enforced that require women to cover all parts of their body other than their face and hands. Men are forbidden to have long hair or wear short coats. Women's rights under the new regime have been severely limited. Women require their husband's permission to leave the house. The clerics have ruled it un-Islamic for women to attend sporting events—such as soccer—where men's legs and arms are exposed. Men and women are not allowed to walk or congregate together unless they are married or related. Many books, especially works of fiction, are banned. Journalists criticizing

Iranian women register to vote at a polling station in Tehran during the second round of Iran's 2008 parliamentary elections.

the government are often arrested, jailed, and some-times executed.

In addition to strict social codes, Iranians are faced with increasing poverty. Inflation is very high, meaning prices are rising too fast. In addition, there is a shortage of jobs. Corruption is common in the management of Iran's abundant natural resources (oil and gas). Suicide is the second most common cause of death in Iran, particularly affecting young women.

Life for the average Iranian is not easy. However, in stark contrast with the average Iranian, clerics enjoy a life of privilege and relative wealth in Iranian society. They have a clear advantage in getting governmental jobs. Their children attend the best schools. When they break the law, they get tried by other clerics behind closed doors. In many respects, clerics seem to be out of touch with the general population, especially Iran's young people, who were not even born when the values of the Islamic Revolution were established.

Clerics seem to be losing their prestige among average Iranians. In the 1980s, they enjoyed great respect and courtesy. Nowadays, however, they are often mocked—as, for example, in the movie *The Lizard*. Fearing ridicule, clerics sometimes change into normal clothes if traveling outside their madrassas.

Their recent unpopularity is not helped by frequent scandals involving senior clerics. Clerics have been a target of anger regarding Iran's difficult economic situation and widespread poverty. Nearly 40 percent of the country's non-oil sector is controlled by *bonyads*, the charitable religious foundations

Jalaledine Taheri, a prominent ayatollah, is shown in 1999. He resigned from the government in 2002, complaining of chaos and general corruption at all levels of religious power in Iran.

maintained by the clerics. Recall that one of the pillars of the Muslim faith is zakah, or giving to charity. Bonyads act as collection agencies for that money. Certain foundations are estimated to be worth around $100 billion. In recent years, reports of fraud and corruption have eroded the public confidence in the way this money is being used. This further damages the already strained relationship between average Iranians and the ruling clerical elite.

# Chapter Six

# Foreign Policy

A t the outbreak of the revolution in 1979, the
victorious clerics declared their intent to spread
the revolution across the Middle East. They regarded
many of their neighbors with hostility and criticized
nations like Saudi Arabia, Bahrain, and Kuwait. Clerics
gave impassioned speeches urging Iranians to support
their Shia brothers in Lebanon. They also urged the
overthrow of Saddam Hussein in Iraq.

Members of the United Nations Security Council convene to vote on new
sanctions against Iran in March 2007.

Many of these policies backfired. The most obvious was in challenging Iraq. In September 1980, Iraq invaded Iran, beginning a brutal eight-year war. Iran found itself short of allies. Most of the Gulf States sided with Iraq, fearing that Islamic militants might try to topple their governments, too.

In 1980, Islamic revolutionaries overthrew the government of Afghanistan and attempted to start their own Islamic republic. Iran, however, was helpless to offer meaningful assistance. Soon, Russia invaded Afghanistan in an effort to support the old Communist regime. Iran, already caught in a war with Iraq, dared not openly confront powerful Russia at the same time.

Thousands of Iranians watch as coffins are driven through Tehran in 1995 as part of a funeral service for Iranians killed in the Iran–Iraq War.

# A New Direction

Following the end of the Iraq war (1988) and the death of Ayatollah Khomeini (1989), Iran began a new type of foreign policy. This one was more practical and less aggressive toward its neighbors. For example, in the 1990s, the clerics adopted a hands-off policy when Muslim militants in Russian Chechnya and Azerbaijan began wars for independence and the creation of potential Muslim states. They dared not risk offending their allies Russia and Armenia. In these situations, the clerics remained mostly silent in their pulpits, choosing to ignore the situations. With regard to Russia, this tactic worked out well. Russia became one of Iran's most important international allies, instrumental in the development of Iran's oil and natural gas industry.

One aspect of foreign policy that the clerics have never ignored is supporting groups dedicated to the destruction of Israel. Hezbollah, based out of Lebanon, owes much of its existence to Iran. When Israel invaded Lebanon in 1982, the government of Iran sent money and a small military force into Lebanon. This small force, part of the Iranian Revolutionary Guard, trained the first fledgling members of the newly formed Shia group, Hezbollah.

Since that time, clerics across Iran have urged their congregations to donate money for Hezbollah's cause. These funds filtered through networks to other clerics in Lebanon, contributing to Hezbollah's significant growth. In 2006, the organization was able to defend itself against Israel's attack, winning acclaim across the Muslim world. The organization operates schools and hospitals, and it provides living expenses for its dead members' families. The United States considers Hezbollah a terrorist group. It accuses Hezbollah of purposely killing civilians (which Hezbollah argues against) and actively promoting suicide bombing. This position by the United States only reinforces the Iranian clerics' commitment to continue its support.

The situation with the Palestinian group Hamas is similar. Although Iran's support for the Palestinian anti-Israeli group has really blossomed only since 2000, the tactics are the same. The Iranian government gives a range of weapons and financial aid, and the clerics whip up popular support and donations, which are filtered into the Gaza Strip.

But as long as Iranian clerics focus their anger primarily on Israel and the United States, Iran as a nation finds itself in better relations with its neighbors in the Middle East. It also finds itself building important relationships with neighbors to the east, including Russia, China, India, and Pakistan. These new allies can help support Iran in the United Nations during its many contests against the United States.

## America and the Clerics

As far back as the 1950s, Iran was an important U.S. ally. American presidents had long supported the shah, and the shah had a reputation for following U.S. advice. Then, in 1976, the new U.S. president, Jimmy Carter, began to criticize the shah for his policies of censorship and his record of human rights violations. At the end of the day, though, the shah was a crucial Middle Eastern ally, and Carter continued to support his regime.

## The Iran Hostage Crisis

When the revolution came in 1979, the Carter administration took a wait-and-see approach. Some advisers urged President Carter to use American military might to put the shah back in power. Carter refused. When the sick shah fled Iran and asked for entry into the United States for cancer treatment, Carter refused this, too. He wanted to remain neutral. Finally, Carter was talked into letting the shah into the United States. A damaging chain reaction followed.

Islamic militants in Iran were furious that America would give refuge to the shah. They wanted him returned to Iran to face trial for alleged crimes he committed during his reign. For Iranians, the decision to allow the shah into the United States confirmed that their former leader was indeed an American puppet. They took to the streets, burning American flags and chanting "Death to America!" At the same time, many Iranians feared that America might move to overthrow their new government. So, on November 4, 1979, a group of students calling themselves Imam's Disciples went on the offensive. They stormed the American embassy in Tehran and took fifty-two Americans hostage. They would hold the hostages for well over a year.

Americans were shocked and angry. Diplomatic relations were broken off, and the United States imposed economic sanctions. Under these sanctions,

A blindfolded female American hostage is led outside of the American embassy in Tehran on November 5, 1979, at the start of the hostage crisis.

no company was allowed to buy or sell Iranian goods. The government seized billions of dollars of Iranian money held in American banks, much of it belonging to Iran's clerics. A hostage rescue mission was attempted, but it failed miserably. Finally, 444 days after the beginning of the crisis, just hours after Ronald Reagan was sworn in as the new U.S. president, the hostages were released.

Relations between the two countries never recovered. For almost three decades now, most of the interaction between the two countries has been con-fined to the arena of the United Nations. Since 2000, the key issues have been Iran's nuclear program and the war in Iraq.

## The United States' and Iran's Nuclear Energy Program

When the shah was in power, the United States was actually eager to help Iran develop its civilian nuclear energy program. Today, however, the United States claims that Iran's regime is using its civilian nuclear energy program to develop nuclear weapons. This would violate international law. Speaking through President Ahmadinejad, Iran's clerics continue to claim that they are developing their nuclear program for peaceful purposes.

The question must be asked: If Iran did, in fact, develop nuclear weapons, would the clerics approve of their use? The clerics say their program is being devel-oped only for peaceful uses. Islam has very specific rules regarding the use of force in wartime, and the

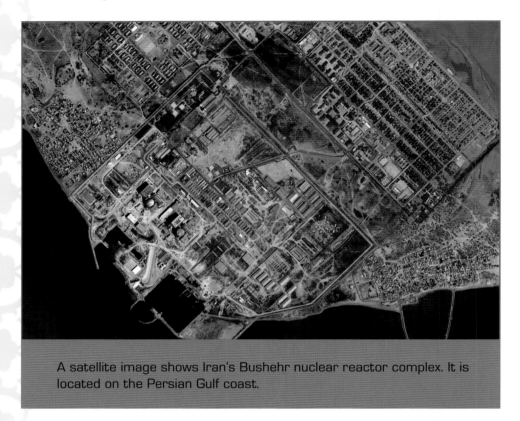

A satellite image shows Iran's Bushehr nuclear reactor complex. It is located on the Persian Gulf coast.

slaughter of innocents is forbidden. At the same time, some high-ranking Iranian clerics claim that Islamic law would allow nuclear weapons to be used to defend Muslims from attack. Ayatollah Ahmad Jannati, the conservative chairman of the Guardian Council, is an example. In a public radio address reported on by AFP News, Jannati stated that Iran should grow into a military superpower for that purpose. "In a not so distant future," Jannati said, "we should reach a point to have the most powerful military equipment in the world so that no one even think about invading our borders."

## Iran and the U.S. Occupation of Iraq

With their extreme secrecy, it is difficult to know exactly how the clerics exercise their influence over Iran's military forces. However, it is clear that very few military operations move forward without the approval of the top clerics. According to the Iranian constitution, the Supreme Leader controls the military and Iran's intelligence operations. He alone has the power to declare war. In addition, he appoints leaders of the Iranian Revolutionary Guard. Among other things, the Revolutionary Guard defends Iran's borders and controls the nation's missile defenses. With its close ties to the clerics, the Revolutionary Guard has become an important tool, both politically and economically.

During the U.S. occupation of Iraq, the United States and Iran again locked horns. American military leaders accused the Iranian military of meddling. Specifically, they claimed the Quds Force, a special unit of the Revolutionary Guard, was training and arming insurgents to do battle with U.S. forces in Iraq. Iran's leaders denied the charge, saying they wanted a stable, secure, democratic Iraq. Finally, in May 2007, the U.S. ambassador to Iraq sat down in Baghdad with his Iranian counterpart to begin a round of diplomatic talks. These were the highest-level discussions between the two countries in twenty-seven years.

Clearly, Iran's global importance is rising. It seems likely that the country's leaders will have to engage in international diplomacy with the Western powers, including the United States. However, it remains to be seen whether the two countries can build on their recent discussions to return to normal diplomatic relations. Even among reformists looking for change, their long Persian heritage and Islamic religion are very important. They do not want to give up Islam and become a secular, nonreligious nation. They may want government to change and they may want the clerics' role in their government to change, but it is clear that they want their Muslim heritage to stay.

# GLOSSARY

**Abu Bakr (c. 573–634)**  Companion and follower of Muhammad; served as the first caliph from 632 to 634.

**ayatollah**  Religious leader among Shia Muslims.

**caliph**  In Sunni Islam, the successor of Muhammad.

**cleric**  Clergyman or learned religious person.

**coup**  Short for coup d'état, a term for the violent overthrow of an existing government by a small group.

**exile**  Living away from one's native country, either voluntarily or by expulsion.

**fatwa**  Opinion issued by an Islamic scholar of law in response to a question or issue posed by an individual or a court of law.

**hajj**  Pilgrimage to Mecca, the birthplace of the prophet Muhammad. All Muslims are obliged to perform the hajj at least once.

**imam**  Spiritual and political leader in the Shia branch of Islam, and direct descendant of the prophet Muhammad.

**impassioned**  Full of emotion.

**Khomeini, Ruholla Mussaui (1902–1989)**  Leader of Iran's Islamic Revolution in 1979 and Iran's political and religious leader until his death in 1989.

**Mecca**  Muhammad's birthplace and the main pilgrimage destination for Muslims.

**meddling**  Interfering; altering something in a secretive or offensive way.

**modernize**  To make up to date; to accept modern ways.

**Muhammad (c. 570–632)**  The prophet of Islam, believed by Muslims to be God's messenger.

**Ottoman Empire** Large Turkish empire that came to control most of the territory in the Balkans and the Middle East. It was established in the early 1300s, and it disintegrated after World War I (1914–1918).

**Pahlavi, Mohammad Reza Shah (1919–1980)** Last shah of Iran, overthrown during the Islamic Revolution in 1979.

**pamphlet** Small, unbound book often passed out to educate the public on a subject of interest.

**Persia** Name foreigners used for Iran until 1935.

**pragmatist** Person with a practical, matter-of-fact way of approaching situations or solving problems.

**Qur'an** Holy book of Islam.

**sanctions** Forbidding of trade or investment with another country.

**SAVAK** Stands for Sazeman-e Ettela'at va Amniyat-e Keshvar; shah of Iran's secret police organization.

*sawm* Fasting; one of the Five Pillars of Islam.

**shah** "King," in Persian; ruler of Iran.

**veto** Power of one branch of an organization or government to block an action or law approved by another branch.

*zakah* Charity that all Muslims are required to give; one of the Five Pillars of Islam.

# FOR MORE INFORMATION

American Iranian Council
20 Nassau Street, Suite 111
Princeton, NJ 08542
(609) 252-9099
Web site: http://www.american-iranian.org
The American Iranian Council (AIC) is a nonprofit and
    nonpartisan educational organization dedicated to
    improved U.S.-Iran relations through dialogue,
    better understanding, and constructive
    engagement.

Embassy of the Islamic Republic of Iran,
    Ottawa, Canada
245 Metcalfe Street
Ottawa, ON K2P 2K2
Canada
(613) 235-4726
Web site: http://www.salamiran.org
The official Canadian Web site of the Iranian embassy
    has news and information regarding Iran, its
    embassy and consulates, and foreign affairs.

Foundation for Democracy in Iran
7831 Woodmont Avenue, Suite 395
Bethesda, MD 20814
(301) 946-2918
Web site: http://www.iran.org
The Foundation for Democracy in Iran is a private,
    nonprofit corporation that promotes a more
    democratic government for Iran.

Foundation for Iranian Studies
4343 Montgomery Avenue
Bethesda, MD 20814
(301) 657-1990
Web site: http://www.fis-iran.org
The Foundation for Iranian Studies is a nonprofit
educational and research institution that aims
to preserve, study, and transmit Iran's cultural
heritage; to study contemporary issues in Iranian
government and society; and to point to the
probable social, economic, political, and military
directions Iran might take in the twenty-first
century.

Iran Heritage Foundation
5 Stanhope Gate
London W1K 1AH
England
Web site: http://www.iranheritage.org
The Iran Heritage Foundation is a nonpolitical charity
founded in 1995, with the mission to increase
awareness about, promote, and preserve the
history, languages, and cultures of Iran.

Middle East Studies Association (The University
of Arizona)
1219 N. Santa Rita Avenue
Tucson, AZ 85721
(520) 621-5850
Web site: http://mesa.wns.ccit.arizona.edu
The Middle East Studies Association (MESA) is a nonpolitical association that fosters the study of the

Middle East and encourages public understanding of the region and its peoples.

## Web Sites

Due to the changing nature of Internet links, Rosen Publishing has developed an online list of Web sites related to the subject of this book. This site is updated regularly. Please use this link to access the list:

http://www.rosenlinks.com/iran/reli

# FOR FURTHER READING

Bauder, Julia. *Is Iran a Threat to Global Security?*
Farmington Hills, MI: Greenhaven Press, 2006.

Cohen, Jared. *Children of Jihad: A Young American's Travels Among the Youth of the Middle East.*
New York, NY: Penguin Group, 2007.

Dumas, Firoozeh. *Funny in Farsi: A Memoir of Growing Up Iranian in America.* New York, NY: Random House, 2004.

Ebadi, Shirin. *Iran Awakening: One Woman's Journey to Reclaim Her Life and Country.* New York, NY: Random House, 2007.

Gheissari, Ali, and Vali Nasr. *Democracy in Iran: History and the Quest for Liberty.* New York, NY: Oxford University Press, 2006.

Johanyak, Debra. *Behind the Veil: An American Woman's Memoir of the 1979 Iran Hostage Crisis.* Akron, OH: University of Akron Press, 2006.

Satrapi, Marjane. *Persepolis: The Story of a Childhood.* New York, NY: Random House, 2003.

Satrapi, Marjane. *Persepolis 2: The Story of a Return.* New York, NY: Random House, 2004.

Seidman, David. *Teens in Iran.* Mankato, MN: Coughlan Publishing, 2008.

Zanganeh, Lila Azam. *My Sister, Guard Your Veil; My Brother, Guard Your Eyes: Uncensored Iranian Voices.* Boston, MA: Beacon Press, 2006.

# BIBLIOGRAPHY

AFP News. "Iran Should Defend Islamic World: Top Cleric." April 8, 2008. Retrieved December 9, 2008 (http://www.breitbart.com/article.php?id= 080418112917.337ttr6z&show_article=1).

Bakhash, Shaul. *The Reign of the Ayatollahs: Iran and the Islamic Revolution.* New York, NY: Basic Books, 1990. Retrieved September 2008 (http://www.questia.com/PM.qst?a=o&d=100368985).

British Broadcasting Corporation. "Exiled Ayatollah Khomeini Returns to Iran." 2008. Retrieved September 2008 (http://news.bbc.co.uk/onthisday/hi/dates/stories/february/1/newsid_2521000/2521003.stm).

Daniel, Elton L. *The History of Iran.* Westport, CT: Greenwood Press, 2001. Retrieved September 2008 (http://www.questia.com/M.qst?a=o&d=100994518).

Daragahi, Borzou. "Iran's Inner and Outer Circles of Influence and Power." *Los Angeles Times,* December 31, 2007. Retrieved September 2008 (http://www.latimes.com/news/nationworld/world/la-fg-circle31dec31,0,1974441.story?coll= la-home-center).

De Bellaigue, Christopher. "Who Rules Iran?" *The New York Review of Books,* June 27, 2002. Retrieved September 2008 (http://www.nybooks.com/articles/15523).

Esposito, John L., Abdulaziz Sachedina, Tamara Sonn, and John O. Voll, eds. *The Islamic World: Past and Present (Vol. 1).* New York, NY: Oxford University

Press, 2004. Retrieved September 2008 (http://www.questia.com/PM.qst?a=o&d=111508006).

Fathi, Nazila. "Film Has Everyone but Clerics Giggling in Iran." *New York Times*, May 5, 2004. Retrieved September 2008 (http://query.nytimes.com/gst/fullpage.html?res=9A04E3DE1E3DF936A35756C0A9629C8B63).

Franssen, Herman. "A Review of US Unilateral Sanctions Against Iran." *Middle Eastern Economic Survey*, August 26, 2002. Retrieved September 2008 (http://www.mafhoum.com/press3/108E16.htm).

Hooker, Richard. "The Caliphate." 1996. Retrieved September 2008 (http://www.wsu.edu/~dee/ISLAM/CALIPH.HTM).

Hoveyda, Fereydoun. *The Broken Crescent: The "Threat" of Militant Islamic Fundamentalism*. Westport, CT: Praeger, 1998. Retrieved September 2008 (http://www.questia.com/PM.qst?a=o&d=107112590).

Hoveyda, Fereydoun. *The Shah and the Ayatollah: Iranian Mythology and Islamic Revolution*. Westport, CT: Praeger, 2003. Retrieved September 2008 (http://www.questia.com/PM.qst?a=o&d=111937876).

Iran Analytical Report. "Politically Entrenched Ayatollahs of Iran: Full Report." February 20, 2007. Retrieved September 2008 (http://www.iranreport.org/Weeklies/02-20-2007.htm).

Malik, Iffat S. "Role of Islam in Post-revolution Iranian Foreign Policy." *Strategic Studies*, 2000. Retrieved September 2008 (http://www.issi.org.pk/journal/2000_files/no_4/article/8a.htm).

Menashri, David. "Iran's Regional Policy: Between Radicalism and Pragmatism." *Journal of International Affairs*, Vol. 60, No. 2, 2007. Retrieved September 2008 (http://www. questia.com/PM.qst?a = o&d = 5020722916).

Menashri, David. "Revolution at a Crossroads: Iran's Domestic Politics and Regional Ambitions (Executive Summary)." Washington, DC: The Washington Institute for Near East Policy, 1990.

Murphy, Kim. "Ctrl + shift as Iranian Clerics Take to Internet." *Los Angeles Times*, April 7, 2007. Retrieved September 2008 (http://articles.latimes. com/2007/apr/07/world/fg-webclerics7).

Siddiqi , Ahmad. "Khatami and the Search for Reform in Iran." *Stanford Journal of International Relations*, Vol. 6, No. 1, 2005. Retrieved September 2008 (http://www.stanford.edu/group/sjir/6.1.toc.html).

Zarif, Mohammad Javad. "Tackling the Iran-U.S. Crisis: The Need for a Paradigm Shift." *Journal of International Affairs*, Vol. 60, No. 2, 2007. Retrieved September 2008 (http://www.questia.com/ PM.qst?a = o&d = 5020722895).

# INDEX

## About the Author

Paul M. Shapera has been working as a youth educator for more than ten years in a variety of settings, including elementary, middle, and high schools. He currently lives in Belgrade, Serbia.

## Photo Credits

Cover, pp. 1, 52, 55, 57 © Atta Kenare/Getty Images; pp. 4–5, 7, 33, 44 © Behrouz Mehri/AFP/Getty Images; pp. 9, 16 Mohammed Sawaf/AFP/Getty Images; p. 13 Abid Katib/Getty Images; p. 17 © James L. Stanfield/Getty Images; p. 19 © General Photographic Association/Getty Images; p. 21 © Popperfoto/Getty Images; pp. 22, 25, 46, 50 © AP Photos; pp. 27, 28 © Keystone/Getty Images; p. 31 © Hulton Archives/Getty Images; p. 35 © Bay Ismoyo/AFP/Getty Images; p. 38 © www.istockphoto.com/Serdar Yagci; p. 41 © Newscom; p. 48 © Michael Coyne/National Geographic/Getty Images; p. 59 © Timothy Cleary/Getty Images; p. 60 © Lauren Maillard/AFP/Getty Images; p. 64 © Bettmann/Corbis; p. 66 © Spaceimaging.com/Getty Images.

Designer: Sam Zavieh; Editor: Christopher Roberts;
Photo Researcher: Marty Levick